March 4. 2001

From someone who lo[...] understands little boys. May you ha[...] pleasure & joy watching your son grow and develop into a man as I have had.

Love,
Mom Asher

What Little Boys Are Made Of

Jim Daly

HARVEST HOUSE PUBLISHERS
EUGENE, OREGON

Boys are found everywhere —

on top of, underneath, inside of,

climbing on, swinging

running around or jumping to....

What Little Boys Are Made Of

Text Copyright © 2000 Harvest House Publishers

Eugene, Oregon 97402

ISBN 0-7369-0268-6

Artwork © Jim Daly by arrangement with Mill Pond Press, Venice, Florida.
For information on art prints by Jim Daly, please contact Mill Pond Press at 1-800-535-0331.

Design and production by Koechel Peterson & Associates, Minneapolis, Minnesota

Scripture quotations are taken from The Living Bible, Copyright © 1971 owned by assignment
by Illinois Bank N.A. (as trustee). Used by permission of Tyndale House Publishers, Inc.,
Wheaton, Illinois 60189. All rights reserved.

WHAT ARE LITTLE BOYS MADE OF, MADE OF?

What are little boys made of?

Snips and snails and puppy dog tails,

That's what little boys are made of.

TRADITIONAL NURSERY RHYME

THERE COMES A TIME

in every rightly constructed boy's

life when he has a raging desire

to go somewhere and dig

for hidden treasure.

MARK TWAIN
THE ADVENTURES OF TOM SAWYER

Jonathan swore to be David's blood brother,
and sealed the pact by giving him his robe,
sword, bow, and belt.

THE BOOK OF 1 SAMUEL

OH, THE EAGERNESS AND FRESHNESS OF YOUTH!

How the boy enjoys his food, his sleep, his sports, his companions, his truant days!

His life is an adventure, he is widening his outlook, he is extending his dominion,

he is conquering his kingdom. How cheap are his pleasures, how ready his enthusiasms!

In boyhood I have had more delight on a haymow with two companions and

a big dog—delight that came nearer intoxication—than I have ever had in all

the subsequent holidays of my life.

JOHN BURROUGHS

HOW BEAUTIFUL IS YOUTH! HOW BRIGHT IT GLEAMS

With its illusions, aspirations, dreams!

Book of Beginnings, Story without End,

Each maid a heroine, and each man a friend!

HENRY WADSWORTH LONGFELLOW

CHRISTOPHER ROBIN WAS SITTING OUTSIDE HIS DOOR,

putting on his Big Boots. As soon as he saw the Big Boots,
Pooh knew that an Adventure was going to happen, and he brushed
the honey off his nose with the back of his paw, and spruced
himself up as well as he could, so as to look ready for anything.

A.A. MILNE
WINNIE-THE-POOH

TWO SMALL ARMS TO HOLD YOU TIGHT,

Two small feet to run,
Two small eyes full of love for you,
One small son.

AUTHOR UNKNOWN

Why God Made Little Boys

GOD MADE A WORLD OUT OF HIS DREAMS,

Of magic mountains, oceans and streams,

Prairies and plains and wooded land.

Then paused and thought, "I need someone to stand,

On top of the mountains, to conquer the seas,

Explore the plains and climb the trees.

Someone to start out small and grow,

Sturdy and strong like a tree" and so

He created boys, full of spirit and fun

To explore and conquer, to romp and run

With dirty faces, and banged up chins

With courageous hearts and boyish grins.

And when He had completed the task He'd begun,

He surely said, "That's a job well done."

AUTHOR UNKNOWN

Little Samuel was growing in two ways—he was getting taller and he was becoming everyone's favorite (and he was a favorite of the Lord's too!).

THE BOOK OF 1 SAMUEL

YOU ARE WORRIED ABOUT SEEING HIM

spend his early years in doing nothing.

What! Is it nothing to be happy?

Nothing to skip, play, and run around all day long?

Never in his life will he be so busy again.

EMILE ROUSSEAU

WHEN THE LAST CRISP SLICE OF BACON WAS GONE,

and the last allowance of corn pone devoured, the

boys stretched themselves out on the grass, filled

with contentment. They could have found a cooler

place, but they would not deny themselves such a

romantic feature as the roasting camp-fire.

MARK TWAIN
THE ADVENTURES OF TOM SAWYER

A Boy's Song

Where the pools are bright and deep,

Where the grey trout lies asleep,

Up the river and over the lea,

That's the way for Billy and me.

Where the blackbird sings the latest,

Where the hawthorn blooms the sweetest,

Where the nestling chirp and flee,

That's the way for Billy and me.

Where the mowers mow the cleanest,

Where the hay lies thick and greenest,

There to track the homeward bee,

That's the way for Billy and me.

Where the hazel bank is steepest,

Where the shadow falls the deepest,

Where the clustering nuts fall free,

That's the way for Billy and me.

Why little boys should drive away

Little sweet maidens from the play,

Or love to banter and fight so well,

That's the thing I never could tell.

But this I know, I love to play

Through the meadow, among the hay;

Up the water and over the lea,

That's the way for Billy and me.

JAMES HOGG

14

THE BOY AND THE FLAG

I want my boy to be the best,

I want him to be great;

I want him in Life's distant West,

Prepared for any fate.

I want him to be simple, too,

Though clever, ne'er to brag,

But, Oh! I want him, through and through,

To love his country's flag.

EDGAR GUEST

To the Boys of America

OF COURSE WHAT WE HAVE A RIGHT TO EXPECT FROM

the American boy is that he shall turn out to be a good American man.

Now, the chances are strong that he wouldn't be much of a man unless

he is a good deal of a boy. He must not be a coward or a weakling, a bully,

a shirk or a prig. He must work hard and play hard. He must be clean-minded

and clean-lived, and able to hold his own under all circumstances

and against all comers. It is only on these conditions that he will grow

into the kind of a man of whom Americans can really be proud.

THEODORE ROOSEVELT

The Inalienable Rights of Little Boys

WE BELIEVE IN THE INALIENABLE RIGHTS OF LITTLE BOYS:

To have mothers who are good pals.

To get dirt on their hands and clothes, to ask questions, to make a healthy racket…

to express themselves and have a place in the sun…

to bring pockets with marbles and nails, and acorns and corks and chalk, and so on.

To learn to laugh at themselves and to take a joke and a hard knock or a disappointment.

To know the world of outdoors—the brooks and trees and birds and flowers—

personally, and in the nature books; to meet those dare-devils, Tom Mix and Rill Hart,

and also the best people of history and literature—Huckleberry Finn, the Knights of the Round

Table, Arnold von Winkelried, Nathan Hale, Robinson Crusoe, and others.

To play at all hearty games and sports—pirates and the Indian and coasting

and ball and skating, and to go swimming in the ol' swimmin' hole.

And to be indulged in half holidays and red roast beef and pink ice cream

and circus parades; and to be spanked—or the equivalent of justice administered,

when necessary—and to be permitted an occasional green apple.

We believe in the inalienable right of little boys to be greatly loved and cared for.

YEOMAN SHIELD

BOYS ARE FOUND EVERYWHERE—

on top of, underneath, inside of, climbing on, swinging from,

running around or jumping to…A boy is Truth with dirt on its face,

Beauty with a cut on its finger, Wisdom with bubble gum in its hair,

and the Hope of the future with a frog in its pocket.

ALAN MARSHALL BECK

"BERTIE SHAKESPEARE DREW…WAS HERE ALL THE AFTERNOON

and sneaked into the kitchen and took the best aluminum saucepan to

use as a helmet. Said they were playing soldiers. Then they made boats

out of shingles and got soaked to the bone sailing them in the Hollow brook.

And after that they went hopping about the yard for a solid hour,

made the weirdest noises, pretending they were frogs."

L.M. MONTGOMERY
ANNE OF INGLESIDE

Boyhood Memory

IT USED TO BE FUN IN THE GOOD OLD DAYS TO RISE AT THE DAWN OF DAY

And dig for worms for a fishing trip. It used to be fun, I say.

For I'll swear that a robin who hovered near knew just what we were about,

Since he flew to the ground where the earth was turned and

begged us to toss one out.

Yes, it used to be fun to go fishing then, but Time has rewritten my terms

Of what pleasure is, and I never get up to dig for a can of worms.

EDGAR GUEST

I'M FISHING.

Don't talk anybody, don't come near!

Can't you see the fish might hear?

He thinks I'm playing with a piece of string;

He thinks I'm another sort of funny thing,

But he doesn't know I'm fishing—

He doesn't know I'm fishing.

That's what I'm doing—

Fishing.

A.A. MILNE
NOW WE ARE SIX

AND HE GREW

and grew strong as a boy

must grow who does not know

that he is learning any lessons, and

who has nothing in the world to

think of except things to eat.

RUDYARD KIPLING
THE JUNGLE BOOK

Here is my description of a truly happy land...

Sons vigorous and tall as growing plants...

THE BOOK OF PSALMS

A BOY IS A PIECE OF EXISTENCE

quite separate from all things else and deserves

a separate chapter in the natural history of man.

HENRY WARD BEECHER

"LOOK," SAID CORIN. "DROP FROM THIS WINDOW ONTO THE ROOF OF THE VERANDAH.

But you must do it lightly, on your toes, or someone will hear you. Then along to

your left and you can get up to the top of that wall if you're any good at all as a climber.

Then along the wall to the corner. Drop onto the rubbish heap you will

find outside, and there you are."

"Thanks," said Shasta, who was already sitting on the sill. The two boys

were looking into each other's faces and suddenly found that they were friends.

C.S. LEWIS
THE HORSE AND HIS BOY

I WAS SO PLEASED AT GIVING THE SLIP TO LONG JOHN,

that I began to enjoy myself and look around me with some interest on the

strange land that I was in…I now felt for the first time the joy of exploration.

ROBERT LOUIS STEVENSON
TREASURE ISLAND

I SUPPOSE THERE'S A TIME IN PRACTICALLY EVERY YOUNG BOY'S LIFE

when he's affected by that wonderful disease of puppy love. I don't mean

the kind a boy has for a pretty little girl that lives down the road.

I mean the real kind, the kind that has four small feet and a wiggly tail,

and sharp little teeth that can gnaw on a boy's finger; the kind a boy can romp

and play with, even eat and sleep with.

WILSON RAWLS
WHERE THE RED FERN GROWS

WHEN I WAS A SMALL BOY IN KANSAS,

a friend of mine and I went fishing...I told him I wanted to be a real major league baseball player, a genuine professional like Honus Wagner. My friend said that he'd like to be the President of the United States. Neither of us got our wish.

DWIGHT D. EISENHOWER,
THIRTY-FOURTH PRESIDENT OF THE UNITED STATES

GOD MADE THE LITTLE BOYS FOR FUN, FOR ROUGH AND TUMBLE TIMES OF PLAY;

He made their little legs to run and race and scamper through the day.

He made them strong for climbing trees, He suited them for horns and drums,

And filled them full of revelries so they could be their father's chums.

EDGAR GUEST

As the boys grew, Esau became a skillful hunter,
while Jacob was a quiet sort who liked to stay at home.

THE BOOK OF GENESIS

A BOY'S WILL IS THE WIND'S WILL,

And the thoughts of youth are long, long thoughts.

HENRY WADSWORTH LONGFELLOW

THE STALLION CHARGED BACK AT THE BOY,

again swerving when he was almost on top of him. For ten minutes Henry watched

the strangest game he had ever witnessed. And slowly he began to understand

the strange understanding that had grown up between this wild stallion and the boy.

A few minutes later Alec came up to him. His shirt was wet with sweat and his blue eyes

glistened with excitement. "Do you see, Henry," he exclaimed, "he just wanted to play!

Look at him, Henry—did you ever see anything so great in all your life?"

WALTER FARLEY
THE BLACK STALLION

ONE OF THE BEST THINGS IN THE WORLD IS TO BE A BOY;

it requires no experience, but needs some practice to be a good one.

CHARLES DUDLEY WARNER

A Boy's Rule for a Happy Life:

If you want a happy, good life, keep control of your tongue,

and guard your lips from telling lies. Turn away from evil and do good.

Try to live in peace even if you must run after it to catch and hold it!

THE BOOK OF 1 PETER

SEVEN-YEAR-OLD ABE WALKED FOUR MILES A DAY

going to the Knob Creek school to learn to read and write....

The schoolhouse was built of logs, with a dirt floor, no window,

one door. The scholars learned their lessons by saying them to themselves

out loud till it was time to recite; alphabets, multiplication tables,

and the letters of spelled words were all in the air at once.

CARL SANDBURG
ABE LINCOLN GROWS UP

BLESSINGS ON THEE, LITTLE MAN,

Barefoot boy, with cheek of tan!

With thy turned-up pantaloons,

And the merry whistled tunes;

With thy red lip, redder still,

Kissed by strawberries on the hill;

With the sunshine on thy face,

Through thy torn brim's jaunty grace;

From my heart I give thee joy,

I was once a barefoot boy!

JOHN GREENLEAF WHITTIER

FISHING WASN'T THE ONLY SUMMER FUN.

Some July evening Father would say: "All work
and no play makes Jack a dull boy. Tomorrow we'll go berrying."
Almanzo didn't say anything, but inside he was all one joyful yell.

LAURA INGALLS WILDER
FARMER BOY

O, WELL FOR THE FISHERMAN'S BOY,

That he shouts with his sister at play!

O, well for the sailor lad,

That he sings in his boat on the bay!

ALFRED, LORD TENNYSON

BOY DEFINED:

Nature's answer to that false belief

that there is no such thing as perpetual motion.

AUTHOR UNKNOWN

O FOR ONE HOUR OF YOUTHFUL JOY!

Give back my twentieth spring!

I'd rather laugh, a bright-haired boy,

Than reign, a gray-beard king.

OLIVER WENDELL HOLMES

"WHAT I LIKE BEST IS NOTHING."

"How do you do Nothing?" asked Pooh, after he had wondered for a long time.

"Well, it's when people call out at you just as you're going off to do it. What are you

going to do, Christopher Robin, and you say; Oh, nothing, and then you go and do it."

A.A. MILNE
THE HOUSE AT POOH CORNER

THE BLUE FAIRY WATCHED HIM RUNNING

and playing in the room, lively and happy as a young rooster crowing for
the first time, and said, "Then my medicine really cured you?"

"It certainly did! It brought me back into this world."

"Then why in the world did I have all the trouble getting you to drink it?"

"That's how we boys are! We're more afraid of medicine than of being sick."

C. COLLODI
THE ADVENTURES OF PINOCCHIO

A BOY, BEFORE HE REALLY GROWS UP,

is pretty much like a wild animal. He can get the wits scared clear
out of him today and by tomorrow have forgotten all about it.

FRED GIPSON
OLD YELLER

Out Fishin'

A FELLER'S GLAD TO BE A FRIEND,

Out fishin';
A helpin' hand he'll always lend,
Out fishin';
The brotherhood of rod and line
An' sky an' stream is always fine;
Men come real close to God's design,
Out fishin'.

A feller isn't plotting schemes,
Out fishin';
He's only busy with his dreams,
Out fishin';
His livery is a coat of tan;
His creed, to do the best he can;
A feller's always mostly man
Out fishin'.

EDGAR GUEST

THOUGH LITTLE, I'LL WORK AS HARD AS A TURK,

If you'll give me employ,

To plow and sow, and reap and mow,

And be a farmer's boy.

AUTHOR UNKNOWN

HE FELT VERY CLEAN AND GOOD, AND HIS SKIN FELT SLEEK

in the fresh, warm clothes. It was the Saturday-night feeling.

It was pleasant, but Almanzo didn't like it well enough to take a bath for it.

If he could have had his way, he wouldn't have taken a bath till spring.

LAURA INGALLS WILDER
FARMER BOY

LITTLE MASTER MISCHIEVOUS, IN THE COOKIE JAR,

Who has ever told you where the cookies are?

Now your sticky fingers smear the curtains white;

You have finger-printed everything in sight.

There's no use in scolding; when you smile that way

You can rob of terror every word we say.

EDGAR GUEST

My Bed Is a Boat

MY BED IS LIKE A LITTLE BOAT;

Nurse helps me in when I embark;

She girds me in my sailor's coat

And starts me in the dark.

At night, I go on board and say

Good-night to all my friends on shore;

I shut my eyes and sail away

And see and hear no more.

And sometimes things to bed I take,

As prudent sailors have to do;

Perhaps a slice of wedding-cake,

Perhaps a toy or two.

All night across the dark we steer;

But when the day returns at last,

Safe in my room, beside the pier,

I find my vessel fast.

ROBERT LOUIS STEVENSON
A CHILD'S GARDEN OF VERSES

The Boy and His Dog

A BOY AND HIS DOG MAKE A GLORIOUS PAIR,

No better friendship is found anywhere,

For they talk and they walk and they run and they play

And they have their secrets for many a day,

And that boy has a comrade, who thinks and who feels,

Who walks down the road with a dog at his heels.

He may go where he will and his dog will be there,

May revel in mud and his dog will not care,

Faithful he'll stay for the slightest command

And bark with delight at the touch of his hand;

Oh, he owns a treasure which nobody steals

Who walks down the road with a dog at his heels.

No other can lure him away from his side,

He's proof against riches and station and pride;

Fine dress does not charm him and flattery's breath

Is lost on the dog, for he's faithful to death;

He sees the great soul which the body conceals,

Oh, it's great to be young with a dog at your heels!

EDGAR GUEST

NO ONE IS GOING TO CATCH ME, LADY,

and make me a man. I want always to be a little boy
and to have fun.

JAMES M. BARRIE
PETER PAN

AH! HAPPY YEARS!

Once more who would not be a boy!

LORD BYRON

Don't let anyone think little of you because you are young. Be their ideal…
be a pattern for them in your love, your faith, and your clean thoughts.

THE BOOK OF 1 TIMOTHY